Jazz Music

Jazz Music

Poems in the Rhythm of Life

Tom Banks

SUNSTONE
PRESS

SANTA FE

Sunstone books may be purchased for educational, business, or sales promotional use.
For information please write: Special Markets Department, Sunstone Press,
P.O. Box 2321, Santa Fe, New Mexico 87504-2321.

Book and Cover design › Vicki Ahl
Body typeface › Perpetua
Printed on acid-free paper
∞

Library of Congress Cataloging-in-Publication Data

Banks, Tom, 1948-
    [Poems. Selections]
    Jazz Music : Poems in the Rhythm of Life / by Tom Banks.
        pages cm
    ISBN 978-0-86534-956-8 (softcover : alk. paper)
    I. Title.
    PS3602.A663J39 2013
    811'.6--dc23
                            2013018754

WWW.SUNSTONEPRESS.COM
SUNSTONE PRESS / POST OFFICE BOX 2321 / SANTA FE, NM 87504-2321 /USA
(505) 988-4418 / ORDERS ONLY (800) 243-5644 / FAX (505) 988-1025

For Diane—

The one who nurtured
my dream
for me
until I could begin to
believe in it myself.

Contents

A Couple of Musings	11	For the World is Breaking Apart	45
A Few Possibilities	12	Forgiveness	46
A Lonely Dog in Winter	13	Fortunate Ones	47
A Place by the Lake	14	Glimmer	48
A Place Past Anger	15	Going Downward	49
A Production	16	Goodbye	50
A World Vision	17	High Desert Sensations	52
Abandon	18	High Desert Winter—A Gray Day	53
About Our Times	19	I'm Sorry, but I was Drunk	54
Across the Bridge of Hope	20	Imagining Tea	55
Addressing My Heart	21	In Dreams of Mine	56
After the Storm	22	In the End	57
All or Nothing	23	Inseparable Souls	58
An Absurd Monk	24	It Might Take 'til Sixty	59
An Eternal Child	25	It Takes so Long	60
An Unusual Lull	26	Jazz Music	61
And Autumn Came	27	June Night	62
Approaching Break-Even	28	Karmic Debt	64
Attaining the Tao	29	Learning to Believe	65
Befriending Myself	30	Lines	66
Below the Desert	31	Love on a Rainy Day	68
Birth of an Artist	32	Miracles	69
Breaking Even	33	Monday Morning, Eight AM	70
Changes	34	Morning of Old Age	71
Changing Seasons	35	Morning Star	72
Communion	36	My Journey	73
Dark Windows	37	My Soul	74
Demons	38	My Worlds	75
Disconnected	39	Near the End	76
Dreamscape	40	New Mexico Roses	77
Drifting	41	New Mexico Snow	78
Dust and Water	42	New Morning	79
Faith and Knowledge	43	Nobody Reminds Me of You	80
Fate Travel	44	Of All the Ways	81

On the Next Rainy Day 82
Opportunity 83
Our Garden 84
Outside World 85
Part of a Star 86
Putting Myself Back Together 87
Requiem 88
Road to Taos 89
Sailing the Sea of Life 90
Saturday 91
Shadow of Doubt 92
Soliloquy 93
Something Out There 94
Soul Mate 95
Southward Goes the Road 96
Summer Leaves 97
Taos Mountain 98
Taos Sunrise 99
Taos, Long Ago 100
The Angel Behind the Door 101
The Big Bang 102
The Dance 103
The Earth Cries 104
The End of Change 105
The Force of Fate 106
The Gardens 107
The Heart Tells No Lies 108
The Lonesome Valley 109
The Mystery 110
The Outcome 111
The Painter 112
The Pilgrimage 114
The Road Home 115
The Road to Serendipity 116
The Truth about Truth 117
The Unknowing Me 118
The Weight of the World 119
The Whole of Me 120

The Whole Truth 121
The Wisher of Wishes 122
The Word Chest 123
Things I've Never Felt 124
This Old Taos House 125
This Road Leads Toward the
    Eternal Sea 126
Thoughts or Wild Horses? 127
Time: The Great Illusion 128
Touched by the Mystery 129
Unlikely 130
Until Winter Comes 131
Visitor in the Desert 132
Warmth 133
Was the Buzz Worth This? 134
Watering the Weeds 135
What Did I Do This Season? 136
What Do I Ask? 137
Where Am I? 138
Where Did the Ideal Go? 139
Where Life is Going 140
Who are You? 141
Why Did Love Go? 142
Wind, Clouds and Mountain 143
Wisps of Thought 144
Without Secrets 145
Yellow Lustre 146

A Couple of Musings

Though only another calendar page,
The fresh air of the New Year wafts in.

What is it about the human psyche,
That relishes change, even when forged?

Can we ever be at peace in one place?
Can we never have it be just good enough?

We are judged—and by others, too.
Why do we grant ourselves, or they,

The power to summarize us so?
We grant the world its eccentricities,

Why not ourselves, as well? Or, is it
That we've lost a sense of who we are?

But we listen, none-the-less, when
Strange voices bring to bear their

Wrath upon our poor, meager souls.
If I'd become the man I wanted to be,

They'd have their troubles finding me
Guilty of being less gracious than they.

A Few Possibilities

For everything that's happened something hasn't happened:
You can see the reminders of this in each other person's life.
But you are yet another person; the you that wasn't,
Or hasn't been, yet; or may never be.

Going on as you are is the bravest way, (and the only way to
See what could be). To change would keep you from finding out.
Experience seems the more reliable indicator of a sort-of-reality;
It doesn't lie, or make things up.

Like a gambler, believing he is on the verge of a big lucky streak,
You must keep in the game: It is the only way to see the truth.
And, when your big win comes, you'll thank the stars that you
Forged on. Then you'll know.

A Lonely Dog in Winter

A lone dog howling,
Calling—awakens me,
On such a cold, clear
Winter night.

I know, by experience
Of winters past, sleeping
In the icebox room of
This old Taos house,

That the temperature outside
Is well south of zero—
And, that the stars and moon
Are bright in the black night.

I know I've heard him
Before, many times even.
And always he calls from
The East—toward Taos Pueblo.

I must get myself up;
Throw on my winter
Vest, cap, and an old jacket,
And go out into his night.

The stars and moon are as
Cold as crystal; and I fear
His piercing bark might
Shatter them all over the heavens.

And then, nothing—silence:
As always, he is not there long.
He has moved on, into the darkness;
And the night continues, without him.

A Place by the Lake

We came to sit by the meadow lake.
Our picnic of red wine and ripe cheeses,
Carried in that rough old woven basket—
The one we bought from the gypsy woman
Who sold her crafts at the Saturday bazaar;
In that little fishing village near the seacoast.

The sky was azure; and the clouds multihued:
With restless shades of gray, black, and white.
The clouds formed many objects. We took into
Guessing what they were; and so often agreeing.
A mild breeze blew through your soft, flaxen hair;
And then you blinked at a fleeting wink of sunlight.

The sun, shining in your eyes, gave to them
A magical radiance—elusive greens and blues;
And something else, too. I had to catch my breath.
I remember the sweet scent of the spring hay. And you—
Timeless beauty, endless grace. You recall, too; I know it.
I'm so sure of this: We've been here before, in another time.

A Place Past Anger

You've never been where you wanted to go;
All those lovely places on the multi-colored map.

You visited many of them, but never found the right one;
The city, or field, that suited your sensibilities (for long).

Now the mature you knows where to go—and it's not on the map.
It's called "A Place Past Anger," and it's in your soul.

No need to travel, and no need to worry about provisions.
Just take your friends and go. Go now! That place awaits you.

A Production

Everything in consonance!
(No need pushing—
It all happens by itself.)
I awake, the next day, to
All that went the night before.
I tried so hard, and gave my all.
How it was for them? I can't know,
But, for me, it was glorious.

A World Vision

Seeing is only one way
Of sensing the world;

And, not even the major one—
Among all the other possibilities,

Both known or imagined—
And even the unimaginable.

Let me not pray to be saved from feeling cold,
Or being hungry, or afraid:

Let me hope for the strength, the resolve,
The fortitude of contentment, to keep going on,

Through all these troubles—
With the attitude of a happy child.

Abandon

Deep chasms on the mountainside,
Where only shadows call.
They'll never feel, in that darkness,
The warm days of spring and fall.

About Our Times

We've had some times,
You and I;
Me being me, and you being you.

We moved along those many roads,
Going from place to place,
With lots of cats; hoping it would all work out.

You left your world,
And I left mine;
(I always felt the change was thornier for you.)

Anyhow, we're here now;
And we're not going anywhere else, just yet.
With nine cats, and no illusions,

The world doesn't seem so big anymore.
Those far-flung shores are the borders, now,
Of this place we call our home.

Across the Bridge of Hope

The bridge of hope—from Washington into Oregon,
On Highway 101—(or from any point to another place).

On hopes and dreams and smiles and tears,
Beyond the wishes and soft goodbyes,

Desire would soar ahead of our hearts,
As we moved on toward adventure, despite our fears.

We found it best to look ahead—but not too far.
And then to look behind—but not too much.

Setting off to seek our fortune, our special place:
Or was our treasure yet to be mined from our dreams?

Addressing My Heart

I spoke some heart-felt words,
But to whom?

I'd addressed, for the first time,
My own heart.

It answered, saying, "Welcome,
I've been waiting."

My heart swelled inside my chest.
I felt the gushing as

The blood came rushing into my
Limbs and head!

How could it have taken so long for
Me to realize that

The heart is the *sine qua non*:
The reason we live.

Not one mortal knows exactly
Why, or how, it keeps on beating.

Or what (or whom), started it:
It just *wished* to become.

Now I am in direct contact with it.
And now, at last, I have a church.

After the Storm

And the sun came back,
After that storm that seemed
It would darken the sky forever.

When I saw it, shining through,
My eyes filled with tears
To know that it was just for us—

A message of renewal.
An answer to a prayer,
Yet unspoken.

All or Nothing

I am not ready to give
All to the world.

And anything between all and nothing,
Will bring about my downfall.

I must remain in the cave
For just awhile longer.

One day I'll plunge into the river,
However rapid and frightening it is.

Once the world becomes
A bit more forgiving,

I must come out—
For God only whispers

Loudly enough
For a cat to hear.

Once all my thoughts,
All of these words,

Are reduced to just a few,
I'll speak again.

The truth in what I say will then
Be known. And all will see

That the best shines
Out of it, and out of me.

And those who have known me before
Will see it more than the new.

An Absurd Monk

(Without Religion)

He is a monk, of sorts.
He ponders life, pointlessly.

So much of each day,
Taken up in thought—but not searching.

Deep thought—about
"How it is," and "What's

Going On?" Not knowing
Why, or how to stop.

Sometimes from these
Trances, comes a poem.

He is limited, in many
Ways, with his writings:

He cannot hold onto
A thought for long.

And, if he tries too
Hard, the words grow

Banal—and he quits.
Only in short spurts does

Anything—words or speech—
Come out understandable.

But then he is not seeking
To be clear. It just comes

As it does, and becomes
What it becomes.

An Eternal Child

Life, a long and tortuous
Series of unsolvable mysteries.

Then one day you find
That the test is over.

And all this time you've run the maze—
Nothing as it appears.

And you, all the time
Trying to make sense of it.

An eternal child, you never gave up,
Or gave in—

And won't,
Right up to the end.

An Unusual Lull

An unusual lull has fallen over my mind today.
Is it the world taking me away?

Away from romanticizing; away from the
Invisible treasures that make it all worthwhile?

But I have learned a trick or two in my advancing age.
The lull is just as exotic, and equally enchanting,

As a spring rain is—or a trip to Neptune.
It is the space between seconds they tell of in The East.

The wonderful stillness that we came from, once upon a time.
And I'm enveloped in it all. And I am living eternity, just for a while.

And Autumn Came

It's a Sunday afternoon in autumn;
Autumn of the year, and the autumn of life.

The chill hovers, and, at sunset, descends
Upon us, like a chilly blanket; not frigid yet.

But the cold is on its way, and sooner than we think.
We only thought we knew about late fall, and winter;

They always came before we expected them to.
I promised you, and myself, we'd be ready this year;

The note I wrote you—to explain—blew away
While I was gazing at the clouds, saying goodbye.

And then a butterfly passed by, and I forgot again;
And thought about him, going where he goes for the winter.

How easily my mind forgets itself when I see butterflies.
The butterfly—my totem, my fetish; my future?

Approaching Break-Even

As the scale falls into balance,
Your heart slows;
And begins to take over your brain.

Now you're in touch—though weakly—
With "The What Is,"
Learning—nascent knowledge—begins.

Was I trying to take too much?
Or, did I try to please too much?
(Or, did I want too much for pleasing?)

Anyway, it all seems moot here.
Not so many questions anymore;
Only what is a treasure—and what is not?

Attaining the Tao

How inevitable it must have been
That I find myself right here.

The struggle, from somewhere to here,
Proves it. And yet I feel like an embryo,

Of some unknown beauty, without
Description in the world I've known.

Personal history—memory—becomes
Unreliable, once you feel yourself

The narrator telling the story of yourself.
If asked whether you ever attained The Tao

Would you, now, be so quick to
Say, "No?"

Befriending Myself

Slowly, glacier-like,
I begin to see myself
As a friend.

Another soul, within
My own, that I am now
Just meeting;

To discuss some old
Matters, and mend
Some fences.

We lived so close,
And saw each other's
Ways, largely with

Contempt.

But now it's like
Another day—we're
Speaking,

Trying to work things
Out so that we can carry
Our friendship

30   Into old age.

Below the Desert

Under the hard *caliche;*
Just a few centimeters down,

Lies, curled up, fetus-like,
Multi-colored balls of life,

Ready to emerge, if spring
Allows; and join their mother.

Remove the first layer of dust,
And, imagine a sheet of glass,

Spread-out over the desert floor:
And see the life, waiting, hoping.

Birth of an Artist

It finally came that an artist passed thru:
From trying to make a living with art,

To there being no living
Without it. A sort of death.

Dying to one life, to begin another. It's the right religion
For a soul that longs to create.

A religion of words painting scenes of thoughts
In all colors and shapes.

Sentences singing songs of traditions. And memories,
Cherished through the ages, worshipped as rituals.

Breaking Even

The best that a gambler can do—break even.
The game was what it was all about, anyhow.

You have reached a level of being
Which is now ruled by the Law of Fate.

I hope future "contact"
Is as direct.

How can I tell a story
When I don't understand it?

I guess I'll talk
About not understanding,

And how it seems so natural to me,
Though I continue to be uneasy with it.

When I learn to accept, even embrace it,
I might understand the big game.

Changes

Take in the form of all you see:
It will not be the same again.
Though it seems to last a lifetime past,
That's not very long at all.

I set off long ago,
To find a new land.
It's a long, long time now;
And almost close enough to touch.

I'm blessed with a wonderful guardian angel.
(I only hope she's durable.)
Then you come to believe it was all just a dream—
No substance to it at all. Of course it was!

Something—a time like that—could only be in a dream.
Where else do gifts get laid at your doorstep,
And no bill comes? And you,
You hadn't the grace anyway.

I've bided my time up until now,
Taking in what there was to see.
Every place, every face—
Shaping the way I came to be.

All this time I learned one thing:
That this world is always changing.
And that no force, or prayer, can help us
Make sense of this rearranging.

Changing Seasons

The seasons changed rapidly
That year—
And then back again,
Before their time,

Confusing us all.
And those that
Count on spring being
Spring were hurt the most.

So I started to
Think of spring,
And the soft, green
Mood it would bring.

But winter was just starting,
And spring was too far off. . . .
Fall had weakened me—
But I'd made it through.

Communion

Of all things in Nature, the Universe,
(And all that might be), which are we able

To communicate with in a conversation?
Can I, for instance, talk with my cats,

Or a star in the sky, or with the trees and grass?
If I listen with all the powers I possess,

Will I "hear them" when they "speak"?
And, if I do sense that I have heard them,

Can I translate, (if such is necessary),
Rightly, what they told me?

This seems so vitally important, this question!
And yet, I may never truly know the answer.

Life, so full of mystery—no real answers to be had.
If, as my heart believes, the Universe is sweet, then,

It must be that I am the better off for not knowing.
And, since I do not know, I am free to make it all up,

As romantic as I please. And to say,
To me and to others: "It is possible."

Dark Windows

What was gloomy becomes more so
Since you went away.

The nights are filled with things
That make me crazy.

The days I've known with you appear
Something unreal.

And our next meeting is like a
Fairy tale—untrue.

It seems that I was happy once;
In New York, I think.

Or was it just a dream—it seems
Too good to have been.

Another day will dawn for me and
The dark windows will show nothing.

Nothing is my life right now—but I
Will hold on to my beautiful dream.

Demons

I have come to know many demons;
Although I cannot describe one of them

To you. For the most powerful of
Demons do not take material form.

They are but energy fields, made
Up of necessary evils: Making it

Possible for our young minds to
Comprehend goodness. Their

Demon-force might show us
The way to the Heart-of-Hearts.

Disconnected

Would I, looking out upon a freshly-mown lawn,
From inside a suburban house, with all its landscaping,
And other utilities, piped-in, or wired-in, from the street,
Find life the same as when I gaze out at the scrub grass?

Inalienable rights seem alien now; not "just there."
I feel a connection, not to the utility poles, or to the
Other unnatural niceties; but to the whim of Nature:
This place, so far away from comfort, yet so comforting.

Dreamscape

The sun brings out a beautiful feeling in me,
When it comes thru my window

At just the right angle,
And just the right time of day.

It is like going to live in a picture.
The artist has created a dreamscape.

You are the visitor—a permanent visitor.
Get to like it right away! Don't even think about it!

It is best to summarily accept
The reality of the dream.

Drifting

Most days start off with a theme.
Something to think about;
Something to change, or make better
Somehow.

And then there are the other days.
Those that are laid out before me
With nothing but time; and possibilities
Unknown.

It is good to seize those days,
The ones with no goals in sight.
And let them take you, cleanse your
Spirit.

After all, the needs that come with
Each new day appear beyond control.
They might even be predestined—your
Moira.

So, after writing down a reminder to
Yourself to take this all in, relax.
Sit back and look at the sky. Just
Live.

Dust and Water

This body, built with blocks of flesh,
Sinew, and locks of hair;
Of all their colors, dark and fair:
And from all different places.

Blocks, bound together with blood;
Blood mixed with blood;
And something else as well:
A transient soul, with many faces.

This body, handed down through ages,
A long, long, book with many pages.
Some were bums, some were sages;
And made from similar matter.

The blocks, disassembling now,
All is gone, all is done.
The storyline has reached its end,
And the blood reverts to dust and water.

Faith and Knowledge

The long Pilgrimage
Now at its rest.

I'm able to enjoy, once
More, this lovely earth,

In a way I might possibly
Never have been able

To do again, but for this
Traveling of spirit and senses.

The dark outside is about to end;
I know this somehow; but only by

Experience. And experience is
But a protection against The Unknown;

A parting gift, to help quell our fears;
From The One Who Left Us Here.

What is the whirling all about?
So much going on, all at once!

Couldn't we live in a quieter place?
(And we will, by-and-by.)

The longer one stays faithful,
Or the more times, if

There is no time,
The stronger that Faith appears.

Fate Travel

The road was laid out
Before us,
Before we ever thought
To take it.
Before we were born, even.
Every career, every life-stage,
Shorter than the last.
Only a few pursuits went on
For long—or loves.
Each so easily left behind.
Always a new favorite.
And reason—not a factor,
Generally speaking,
In any of the affairs.
But now I know more
About love and things.
I pick my favorites
Well, now they're forever.

For the World is Breaking Apart

And all that going on now! Everything breaking apart,
At a rapid pace, it seems to me; one who has come
From a slow and quiet place.

But would I try to stop it? No.
For I believe in fate and destiny too much to set them off their
Needful track, never to find where we were headed.

Forgiveness

In certain ways, I was never innocent; not as far back
As I can recall, anyhow. And yet, I feel innocent today.

Forgiveness was not necessary, either:
First, there must be a clear transgression.

Becoming innocent is simple:
One only just needs to develop his own definition of sin.

The level of comfort with your new-found innocence will be in direct
Proportion to the verity of your own description of it.

When I look back on the variety of misdeeds I can remember,
I feel pangs of guilt, and regrets aplenty.

But, when recalling the circumstances that lead up to them,
I realize that I almost always had good intentions; or at least not bad ones.

The few exceptions, those which haunt me permanently—
Would probably surprise those who knew me then.

Fortunate Ones

We are born into a fortune;
Mostly squandered by the

Time it's all over. We love,
And find that the beginning

Of love is the beginning of
Sorrow: Worth it all the same.

Worrying, we close out all
That is valuable; and when

The revelation comes, if it
Comes at all, is when we're

Taking in the last of our
Precious breaths—those,

Too, gone now but for faded
Memories of how sweet they were.

And off we go into that
Great beyond;

From where we came.

Glimmer

And, in the end, all that was left
Of life was the glimmer.

Every lovely thing—all that I loved—
Had in it the glimmer.

Had I remembered all
Else but the glimmer sooner,

Would I—could I—have understood
The secret of it all?

All those pretty words—
Too pretty, perhaps, to seem true.

Hold them back a bit. See if
In the words we are found—

But with a less clear view. Not so much
Light on things—only a glimmer.

Going Downward

Slowly I descended into Hell;
(I should have seen the signs.)

By the time I looked about—
Or behind—the sun was lost.

Could I have altered, anyhow,
The master fate, that wrote the lines?

No one is with me on this path.
Can I get back? If so, at what cost?

But then, why return
To what went before?

Except the part that includes her—
My only hope.

Goodbye

So many movements
In that certain direction,

Or was it only a few?
And then a reckoning,

That it all meant something.
And, finally, you said goodbye

To me—and saved me
Saying goodbye to you.

I can't just make everything
Alright again—as much as I want to.

And the pain keeps falling,
Wherever, and whenever, it wants.

Just how much can we expect?
But yet there's still time—

And all we need do is to give in.
Often, a couple is defined by

What it would take for them to part.
Whatever happens will

Probably be tragic, anyhow.
Another in a long line—

And this, too, will pass.
All our imperfections

Forgiven; but when?
In the end, one can't remember

What it was he should've done.
After all, there's no way we could've

Known what could've been.
This isn't the story anyway;

So don't get so serious.
It's all yet to be written——to be lived.

High Desert Sensations

Lovely heat that sears the flesh.
And beautiful cold beyond the skin's
Power to withstand.

These are the mountain plains
And valleys in high
Summer and deep winter.

The strong are spared. . . .

High Desert Winter—A Gray Day

It is a gray day.
The grayness has

Descended upon the
Mountain top—pushing it down,

Onto the lower regions
Where dust clouds blow

Around in the spring gusts.
Soon the heavy weather

Will stay far-north of us;
And the relentless sun will,

Once again, bake the mesa—
Hardening it into a sullen brown.

But first the stage of colors
Will dance by—showing us

How the desert can be—
Though only for a brief moment.

How, then, could we experience it all
In its true glory except in the

Deprivation all the other seasons
Save springtime bring?

I'm Sorry, but I was Drunk

For all those times I would but
Change one thing I did, or didn't do:

One thing that might have made
So much difference in our happiness.

And say to you, "I'm sorry, I was
Drunk." And if you cannot understand,

Or if you are angered by my
Plea, any attempts at explaining myself

Would not help, but only hinder.
Let us leave the tavern now, and climb

To the top of that hill we've always
Wanted to go to; the air is rarified there.

Imagining Tea

Thinking so deeply,
I forgot I was drinking green tea;
And ceased to be aware of anything else.

What was a mindless act, repeated again and again,
Became a singular pleasure; hard to
Believe nothing had really changed.

As I sipped, I stopped
Once more, to look out the west-facing window,
Onto the arid plain; a place we'd come to live.

And wondered, "Why here? Why now?"

Like considering the tea drinking,
I realized all I'd been missing
While my mind was so hard at work.

In Dreams of Mine

My dream life had come alive,
It seemed.

And each night the dreams took on
A reality of their own. Those dreams,

Of strange—not bad—not good—
Situations.

And, I must add, the people weren't bad.
One night I'll go to where the dreams are.

And with those that live there, remain.
I'll fall asleep, like always,

But not wake up to what we know as life.
I became what I became

And didn't become what I didn't.
Each success an imminent failure.

In the End

An endless sequence of chances,
And invitations to dances.

Ten lost years, here and there,
Amount to a life's allotted time.

You'd gone to so many places,
But forgot what took you there.

Why didn't you stay in that
One place, with the moonbeams?

You were so much a part of it:
You wanted it to consume you.

But you gave it up for another
Chance, another wonderment. . . .

You still give up, but not so quickly.
And, in the end, you'll find your place:

At the end of giving up. There's no reason.
It could've been anywhere along the way.

Inseparable Souls

We are plants without roots.
And yet a hundred thousand acres
Of earth are needed for us to grow.

We do not move over the land, or
On it, for that matter—but above it.
The land travels with our movement.

And tomorrow we will be
Joined with another little soul.
He will notice we've aged.

Along with us he'll fly,
Seeing the world in his own way—
And also as we see it—one family.

And then, when this dream ends,
We'll all go somewhere else,
Together as a single soul—inseparable.

It Might Take 'til Sixty

Dreams and desires,
Attempts and misses—

Often accompanied
By a feeling of certainty,

But most times
By doubt and fear.

Fear that you won't
Make it,

When all along, you
Lacked a sense of direction.

In other words, not knowing when,
Or why, you move.

It might take you 'til sixty to begin.
But then desire wanes; and

Truth is always in the way.

The requirements you've always lacked,
But now come more easily.

It Takes so Long

It takes so long to learn anything;
Maybe longer than we have . . .

For, first you have to find your desire;
And, then, the road ahead is so long.

So you decide to just live-it-out,
To accept it as it came.

And yet, the desire
Has opened some windows.

And you have seen out—
Random views, to be sure.

Not a lot to be made of it all.

But, one day, it may
Come to a total—or subtotal;

Like a formula on a
Blackboard, chalked by hand.

Jazz Music

Let my poems
Resemble, in their form,
Jazz Music

Going this way,
And that,
Letting the words do what they'll do.

Seeming at random
And yet, somehow,
Holding together, too.

June Night

The evening light of a June night has a playful way
Of setting your mind astray.

In an instant, your reverie is broken, like a sea shell,
By someone's laugh breaking out of an open doorway.

And you listen, as it dies away, across the timeless stretch
Of open land. It beckons you to follow—

Though it might be on its way over the end of the earth,
Or to scale a rainbow,

Or to ride a river's flow, if you can stay afloat,
To wherever its raging waters go.

And when you get there you'll be free,
No longer feeling the compulsion

Toward fulfilling your potential,
(Or their expectations of you).

To live and die by your own hand,
Your own mind and your own will.

And all this time I've spent away—
Away from my own soul and longings:

Now I know belongings are not, in my tried
And true heart, needed.

You always hovered above them; and me,
Looking down on all our plights.

It's just, with them you moved in shadows—
With me, you move in stark sunlight.

How difficult! The final letting go. But you will land
Softly—more so than I—of this I'm sure I know.

It's all coming apart. Now I feel
The pieces go this way and that in time.

But, all is immortal and everlasting. It runs
The gamut from the ridiculous to the sublime.

To save myself from drowning in the pool, I climb
The short ladder, up and out onto the barren land.

It is cold and gravity works
Much too well out here—but yet I begin to walk,

In a halting gait, across the dunes of shifting sand,
And ever toward a promised land.

The last flavor of the wine in my mouth is washed away,
As I swallow my fate.

Will the wine sweeten again when I least expect it,
Or did I gulp too soon and savor too late?

Life lost control—
So much depended upon others.

Only time, like wine, will tell.
'Til history ends, we all wait. . . .

Karmic Debt

Oh Karma! When will you be paid?
Just as I think my debt is even,
You come back calling here.

I don't even remember all I owe you:
All of the myriad transgressions (I hope intentions count . . .).
But I know you do.

I thank you for the occasional relief;
Those times when I felt so free.
You can be kind, too.

And when the piper calls, I'll tell him,
"I paid The Fates, and now I'm clear:
At least, I hope, for another year."

Learning to Believe

Try to do without it: The Truth.
It will only bring you eternal grief, and exile.

And what is it, anyway? Just you,
Thinking you know something;

Wanting to tell it to all the others.
It is foolish and dangerous—

(I don't care why you are doing it.)
Learn to believe; it is the closest

You are likely to come to truth;
At least on this plane of existence.

And teach others to believe, too.
But in themselves; not in you.

Lines

Lines are what the natural world is.
Some lines seem to stand alone,

While others intersect, or spread to
Meet other lines coming from

Other places in space and time:
And all from the same place.

You have lines, just like me, though
I can see yours more clearly than

You: For there is one less reflection
For me to see through.

Only dreams, it seems, lack lines.
Perhaps there is no focus in dreams,

What eyes do we use then, anyway?
And the shapes and colors are muted;

So like impressionistic scenes where
Only dark light is permitted.

But even in my dreams the shapes
Are lines, of sorts; and are no more

Changeable than the ones I see in
"Reality." (Which *is* made up?)

To create art is to alter the lines to
Suit the purpose, or whimsy, one feels

At any given moment; and desires to
Share with others of his kind—Artists

Seek a reaction. In one way hoping
The observer sees, in this alteration,

Something of the artist's heart and soul;
But all the same, if only it moves him.

The artist is a dangerous magician; he
Never knows if we will get back again.

Lines have shape and color, too. Like
A tree limb. And don't look for lines

That stay the same from day-to-day.
They, like the womb we all inhabit,

Are changing before our very eyes. In
An instant, a blink; all is unlike,

Somehow. Only memory is left behind
(That deceiver!), to make sure we keep

The pain of love alive. In the heart of man
Lay his lines: He sees only in blood.

Love on a Rainy Day

The drops beat down,
Synchronizing with
A thousand hearts—
They, too, with gray
Clouds abounding.
But when the life-lighting
Beams of sun return,
Or the blue-white
Stardust falls
To earth on a clear,
Moon-struck night,
Will my rainy day
Feelings prove true,
Or merely figments
Behind the rain's curtain?

Miracles

Funny, we've been
Talking for so long,
And yet I don't know you.

Millions and millions
Of words, both ways,
And not a hint of meaning.

Are we trying hard enough?
Or too hard? Or are
We just defeated by the

Language?

I speak of miracles—
Which must be all nice,
All good, all beautiful.

And, in their way, they all
Are—mixed in with the
Tragedy, emptiness and

Loss of that love we
Wanted so badly, but
Gave up, in the end.

We need some signs
And symbols—like
Religions use—to make

What we mean—what we
Want—more clear, more real
But first, some time must pass.

Monday Morning, Eight AM

What is it that's left to do,
After all these years of caprice?

Sit and remember? Ruminate?
Try forgetting (except for the lessons)?

Find a creative, productive
Way of making use of it all?

Work on becoming a better man;
Or become at ease with who I am?

Play around with the old habits;
Or try replacing them with new ways?

Or just remain open-hearted,
And see where the river takes me?

Anyway, it's Monday morning.
By afternoon it won't matter so much.

Morning of Old Age

Let us awaken, on that morning of old age,
As if we found ourselves at a campground,
With all the things we'd like to do available to us.

And yet nothing to do at all
But look forward to playing with
Our mutual sensibilities, and open hearts.

The day may start out dreary,
But the sun behind the clouds is still bright enough
To break through before the day is out.

Youth is excess—we can do it all and never tire.
Middle age is like being at a cocktail party, by demand:
One must decide who to be around and what to drink.

And, if we've chosen well our company,
And drank only to satisfy our need to alter,
For just a while, our outlook on life,

We will wake up on that day with bright eyes,
A thankful heart, and a soul filled with memories,
Made exciting by the chances we took on the road
To that place; where memories are made.

But, if we kept bad acquaintance,
And drank beyond our desire to keep some dream alive,
The morning becomes the morning after; and we are woozy,

And think, "I never became what I wanted to be."
And why is it you never became what you wanted to be:
Peculiar chemistry?

Morning Star

The morning star,
A miniature full moon;
But brighter, still, it seems.

Flashing proudly,
Its own light.
Proclaiming an end
To the night, and to dreams.

As she pushes up
The dark curtain,
Below her now
Only shades of blue.

The sun, our own star of life,
Will follow soon.
And tonight, with luck,
The tranquil moon.

My Journey

Like you, I have been journeying,
From place to place, it's true.
But the real journey has been
From looking for truth (reality)
To revealing un-truth (real).

And now, onward, toward that Fate
Which is not within my power.

And, as the material world fades,
(I hope not completely!),
And the world of mystery comes nearer,
Some of what is the sum of me
Dissolves into the quantum realm,

Where it came from, I believe;
Back when I could know these things.

My Soul

My soul was.

Neither time nor space did it occupy.
Only the veiled perception of itself made it real.

It longed to exist in full.

Even with the promise of tragedy, cold and hunger,
It yearned to create a period in which to live.

And so it did.

And that place in time and space,
That my soul brought about

Was a glory to behold.

The only tragedy I experienced,
As it happened, was when, and how

It came to its end.

My Worlds

How many worlds I live in each day!
There is the world of the morning,
And the world of mid-day.

The world of the afternoon,
And of the evening's song,
And the twilight world, so long.

In the morning it's fresh, this world
Of mine. And then I cross the median line,
Into yet another world.

The waning of the day will find
Me covered over with the waxing
Of the morning's dreams, now glazing;

And melting in the heat
Of such a sun that weakens me;
And sets me thinking of tomorrow.

Near the End

The storms didn't come anymore;
And the forest died, and became desert.

The last embers of the last fire ebbed.
Then a wind came from the East;

Setting the coals aglow once more.
What almost died was new again.

It started to rain. And lightning
Was seen in the distant twilight.

New Mexico Roses

Suddenly, the scent of roses filled the air.
And, while that essence was there,
All else was silenced, obliterated.

I could think of nothing else:
Least of all the future.

When that scent became the past,
It was just as sweet, in its memory.

And, when no fragrance was left,
Except the memory of roses (sour, now),

I returned in a dream to those rose-scented days,
A thousand years ago.

New Mexico Snow

The snow came today.
It came on the westerly.
The snow came sideways—
Mesmerizing our cats.

The flakes were lumps,
Like wet bits of powdered sugar.
Before long it was over—
Then the sun shone thru again.

Nature had reminded me to smile.

New Morning

I awakened this morning early,
While the sky was still and cool,
In yet another strange land.

Certain of the sights and sounds
Were familiar. But yet not at all
The same as before sleep.

A bird of prey circled over me,
Riding the first thermals of an
Otherwise bone-chilly day.

He knows this land. It is everything
There is to him. His sanctuary—
It provides all for him.

And it never changes.
To him it is eternal, and will
Remain the same, he would

Hope, if hawks were inclined to
Hope. No, he is sure of all
This—an eternal faith—

Which will never waiver in his
Long lifetime. Only after his flight
To another sky far away

From here, where he can fly
Without the thermals, without
The sun for light to see,

Will he lose his fidelity. He
Will forget all of us he's ever seen,
Even in his deepest and fondest dreams.

Nobody Reminds Me of You

I move among others;
My eyes searching through.
A feeling brushes my soul,
In the way you used to do.

I look around, and see someone familiar,
(At least I wish them so),
But, try as I might, nobody ever
Reminds me of you.

I'll round the next corner,
More hope in my heart;
That in an encounter,
Or the next work of art,

If only just one familiar
Thing they might do;
But nobody ever
Reminds me of you.

I'll notice a semblance
Of your shade of blue;
(Or maybe a tiger-striped
Kitten will mew. . . .)

But it's just as well
That the old times flew.
For no one *could* ever
Remind me of you.

Of All the Ways

Of all the ways
To say the same thing,
Mine is but one.
This keyboard,
This piano of keys,

Where I create music
With my fingers.
Words put to rhythms,
And, sometimes, rhyme.
Songs of my mind;

And who-knows-what else.

On the Next Rainy Day

Next time it rains like this
I'll be ready for it—

There's always a spate of
Sunny weather in-between.

This day snuck up on me,
Caught me unprepared.

For I was asleep for so long;
Unaware of the goodness going on.

Now, just when I need it so,
I've forgotten what it was like,

So long ago.

Opportunity

We saw a chance,
Waving from the deck of a pirate ship
That was going out to sea.

One glance, and a nod,
And we leapt hand-in-hand from the pier.
A giant leap it was!

Tears came down,
As our ship crossed from green water to blue.
Fear became enchantment.

Strangely, we'd thought
To take so many of our treasures with us—
As if we knew we were not returning.

A green light on one side,
And a red light on the other, our ship had.
Foghorns made us shiver.

Our treasures began to shift,
And caused the ship to list.
Now they litter the ocean floor.

We'd lost the lights of port,
So we veered to the right;
Toward the green light.

Somewhere out there in the night,
Beyond the foamy fog bank,
Lay freedom—and yearning.

Our Garden

It is a place apart
From the rest of the earth;

Bordered on all sides—
Only open below, and to the sky.

A place that is soft,
And catches the sun and rain.

Wherein a seed might
Be captured; or planted.

But first, it must be cleared
Of all weeds and rocks,

And then nurtured—
By man, earth and sky.

So that, when all is right,
Something new might emerge.

Outside World

Outside the window,
Where a cat sleeps
On the sill,
Real life is coming down.

Everything *is* life and death
For those creatures
Outside in the open;
Or it is nothing at all.

Somehow they know
That they can count on nature
To either give them what they need,
Or to let them go on.

Either way will do fine.
They count on fortune
To be kind all the time.
They see more than we.

Part of a Star

Grounded and still,
On a high soaring orb.
Enclosed, and yet part of a star.

Locked in a dance
With Heaven and Hell,
Though not here, where we really are.

Putting Myself Back Together

I came apart—
A little here,
A little there,
(Although sometimes
More all at once).

Now I'm picking
The pieces up
And trying to fit
Them together.

The more I try,
The more I find
It is not like a picture puzzle.
There is no right place
For each piece.

And the pieces are
Always the same—
Too familiar.
They came along
From childhood.

So I'll have to
Devise a new puzzle,
Based on the loose
Pieces of me—
And then try again.

Requiem

He called it the end of
His rainbow.
And, perhaps, in the
Truest sense, it was.

How was he, after all,
To know,
That this Utopia would
Serve, also, as

The end of his road?
Listening, now, to the
Silence that only an
End can bring:

Ends of rainbows;
Ends of roads;
Ends of who-knows-what.
I sit; bewildered.

Road to Taos

There's a road that leads to Taos.
It assumes different numbers,

And the signs are many-colored;
But it gets you here all the same.

It just takes longer than
The ones you might pick off a map.

That map is like a body—
And the roads, its veins.

You pass the roadside businesses,
Where those who went before you

Found a place to stay;
Their dreams dot the way.

They'll be here for you,
Always, on your brief stay.

Sailing the Sea of Life

Like an epic sea journey;
Only able to see from horizon to horizon.

Sometimes knowing the mysteries;
Other times bewildered by the simplicities.

Long days without the sun to steer by—
(Or was it the stars you needed?)

Saturday

In the world that has been created,
Let us hope that we will not be afraid,
If alone.

Something wants everything to be this way.
After all, why else should we be here?
Is this reason?

What would it be like if any one little event
Had happened differently,
Or not at all;

When this whole picture can be altered
By the least thought, or action?
So unpredictable!

Objects, if there are any, are being forced
Into their shapes and sizes:
It will all reverse;

Or take some turn at another place
In this mystical continuum. And yet,
Be the same.

But for now, at least, it is all what it is.
And it is lovely, for the most part,
Just as it is.

Shadow of Doubt

The blinding light
Of inspiration

Can be extinguished
By the shadow of a doubt.

(How many realities?
How many shades of light?)

Night leaves us only one—
Unchangeable, silent, unforgiving.

Soliloquy

I attribute some troubles
To others.
That's called humanity.

But they are much too wise,
And real,
To attribute theirs to me.

I am making some progress
Against cynicism,

But before you judge me,
Realize from where I came.

They might even
Have wanted, dearly,
To do me favors;

But, knowing me so remotely,
Couldn't even do that.

Something Out There

Open your door! The wind is calling.
Outside your house the world is going on.

And magic is always in the air.
Some things you can see, and some you can't;

At least, not yet. Not until you learn to read,
To see, and to hear with your heart's senses.

You don't even know what you are guilty of.
Your meager actions are only worthy of your own grief.

Yet, it only looks for you to come closer,
Or at least stay where you are for a while.

You left it for a body, but it still loves you.
So, it wishes you to enjoy even this, that breaks its heart.

After all, you are so young still;
And a ticket sits beside your pillow.

All the others are free because they are useless.
This dream takes a ticket:

This dream will carry you home.

Soul Mate

What shall we ever know about another?
To be intimate, trusting?
To give oneself to another's whims,
And to never, up to the deathbed and beyond,
Find reason to doubt them?
This, then, is the meaning of soul mate.

It is a tragedy of being human,
That your soul mate
Might only be discovered,
As your eyes, gazing upon them
Where their hand locks in yours,
Fade their colors into eternal night.

The finest of the gifts of life is to know yours
At first sight, and to enjoy
Your all-too-brief time with them to its fullest.
In a way it could be said that
The moment of surrender to your soul mate
Is a kind of glorious death:

The death of ordinary life.

Southward Goes the Road

There is a road that leads south.
It also goes east and west;
And northward, later on.

It's a road you pass each day,
On your way to doing things;
Then home. Someday,

You may take that turn, either
Alone, or with your friend.
(What's around the next bend?)

The sun sets in the south for you
On the first few evenings outward.
Then changes positions.

That's not all that will be different—
From now on.

Summer Leaves

Suddenly the wind blows up.
And now, upon the stream's bright surface,

Floating by to the tempo of the wind and water,
The leaves of summer pass before our eyes,

Taking their well-earned curtain call.

Their life has ended: Barren branches;
Soon, to become the trees of winter.

But not until the fall is through,
Having her own Grand Review.

Taos Mountain

We saw the mountain,
And traveled toward her.

The road was wide-open,
For a time and distance.

Wandering the desert,
Staying near to a stream.

New birds were sailing,
Close to the stinging earth.

A heavy sky hung above us:
Clouds like fish in an aquarium.

And then the road ended,
Or split into many paths.

Some lead upward, but
One followed the stream.

And we took that one for a while.
But none led to the mountain anymore.

We go off, now, along with the stream.
Off the mountain, and back toward the sea.

The mountain will call us back soon;
Enticing us to return home, to stay.

Taos Sunrise

The Taos sun rises
Over the saddle in the mountain.

I wish I had my glasses on,
So I might see it clearer.

And then I wonder;
"Am I not seeing it as it is?"

The sky is on fire,
In shades of quiet, and drama.

Blurred and blazing in its promise
To this new day.

Taos, Long Ago

I dreamt I'd lived here long ago.
A time before the coming of many people.

The brown, arid land, the scrub brush, the clouds and sky;
They looked very much the same then,

Save for the dwellings that now dot the landscape.
And the mountain was different then, too:

It was taller, it appeared to me, and had sharper features.
It seemed to have the energetic blood of youth

Coursing through its jagged ledges and valleys.
Now the mountain seems older, softer;

More like weathered green leather:
And with tamer blood now in its veins.

(Perhaps this has something to do with the dwellings,
But anyway. . . .)

I lived here a long, long, time; keeping track of every day:
Not by numbers, or by any calendar; but by naming them.

You see, from sunrise to sunrise, each day is unique.
One only has to look closely to notice that. Try it.

If you find it difficult, naming each day of your life,
Take your time, observe—make finer use of your senses.

The Angel Behind the Door

I found myself before a great door, about to knock;
Not knowing who might answer.

But something held me back: I thought not
To give in to weakness that might be fleeting.

In the next second my own spirit might go to soaring;
And, if it did, I would turn away from the door,

And walk away, without imploring, without appeal—
On my own two feet.

Then the angel on the other side of the
Door smiles, and shakes her head.

Lovingly, she wishes me Godspeed until I come to her at last;
After all the trials and tribulations are done,

Through death's door; where we all
Must come to knock, someday.

The Big Bang

It's morning; the mind explodes.
Tightened-up from a night of dreaming.

It sends its tendrils forth.
Synapses clicking, exploding, generating.

The night has congealed
All that went before; the day before.

And starts, anew, another day;
Another history of all there is, or has been.

The Dance

Life is a dance with no step-patterns,
Or even a partner; much less a leader.

Until you can hear the music as yours,
You won't know how to move to it.

A touch: Is it the touch of another?
You blush, and want to pull back.

(This shouldn't be exciting in the way that it is!
But you can't move away, for fear of losing it.)

After a while you give in and move, too.
How you hope it is alright, but

It will not be either good or bad; now or ever.
It is immune from all that.

Finally you fuse with it. You are now at the dance.
Where were you before?

The Earth Cries

As I was walking
Over the earth,

I heard the earth
Crying.

All kinds of cries—
Ownership,

Distress; Lonely cries—
"Come to me!"

Listen and you will hear, too.
Everything needs something.

And yet they remain unfulfilled—
Most of them, anyhow.

The End of Change

How strange it sounds: "The end of change,"
For something always takes the place of things that end.

And something new has to be something changed,
Does it not? We change, (tho' we might not want to—just yet).

Then we find ourselves again in that new world,
Connected by desire, just as before.

The Force of Fate

Fate is that force
Which keeps flashing
Before us our mysterious
And unintelligible dream.

Driving us onward;
Toward madness, and
Then toward fulfillment,
At its discretion or whim.

Fate speaks to each
Of us, always and forever.
Beautiful and frightening
At once; for we might've

Possessed the power to
Ignore it completely, (save the
Despair involved), for a
Long, long time.

The Gardens

All those seeds we planted;
Hoping to have a garden someday.

One that would sustain our bodies;
And dreams. Tho' the seeds haven't

Grown as we expected them to,
Their shoots are undeniable.

We left them there, in many places, to
Grow on their own; as we knew they would.

Will we forget them? Will they forget us?
Comfort calls, with its deathly whisper.

It wants us to forget; to wait too long.
So that, by the time we return to our gardens

We might lose the sensibilities to recognize
Them; all now gone back to wild.

They will still know us; but will we know them?
And what a tragic loss, if we should forsake

The very places we've prepared for our meeting,
One day. The animals know about all this;

Better than we, or, at least me. . . . So I count on
All of you, my loves, to see me through:

To light the way back to the flowering gardens,
With the speed of angels; while we still have wings.

The Heart Tells No Lies

I recall now how it looked—
Moonlight at midnight.

You were there, too. I knew,
For I was bigger than myself.

I must love you very dearly,
Because I always want you near.

Your approach is always a cause
For celebrating. The speeding up

Of my heartbeats tells that story.
And, the heart tells no lies.

The Lonesome Valley

Once again I find myself here in this valley; alone,
With just my senses keeping me company.

I've walked this way before, many times; both in the
Stark light of day, and in the darkness of night.

The valley stays the same, eternal. This is where the
Answers, such as they are, dwell; I'm certain.

I love coming here, although I avoid it, generally:
Perhaps it's the foreboding I feel when the call comes,

And I leave the safe haven of my naïve reality behind.
But I know the call too well to disregard it—I *must* go.

Once there, I begin to feel at ease, and away from pain.
Then I open up my heart, and ask why I am there.

What matter, this time? What ghosts must I face?
I will not stay here long—I never do: Time is short.

I must return, and take up living in the world again.
But, once back in it, I'm happy. And I know how

Blessed I am to have my valley; my own retreat.
One day I will come to stay in my valley.

Whether I will leave it again, I cannot know.
But, as is the nature all things, I will or I won't.

The Mystery

From here you can feel it;
The breath of a butterfly.
Sweet as a breeze that blows
Over a flower in springtime.

The wispy cloud that glides
Like a cat across the sky.
A certain artwork that catches
The eye, yet unknown.

You are near the mystery now;
Outside, still, but so close as
To be a part of it. Humans, with
But few exceptions, exist outside it.

The mystery is closer than you think.
Right there! You felt it; though
You deny . . . You want to stay
Safe, sane, normal—I understand.

The Outcome

We live a life of ten thousand sorrows, and yet we smile;
For, after all, that is what makes up a life.

If love is natural, why then must we keep learning it?
(Mostly, though, it's fear and repetition).

When the noise subsides, (and that happens at different stages,
Even with the same senses), we will know what is real.

Until then, until the next experience, (which might have all new rules),
I wish you a life all your own.

The Painter

In a dream I was an artist—a painter.
Though I, in my other dream, have not ever

Painted a picture, yet there I was doing that.
I saw a place on my canvas where two lovely

Shades converged, but barely touched: One of
Blue and one of green. The blue was like a

Shard of butterfly wing I once saw as a child.
The green, the feathers of a favorite mallard duck

That once lived on a stream, outside my window.
I took up my brush and, ever so carefully, folded

The blue oil onto the green—and a miracle
Began to unfold! The one color began to absorb

The other, (or both to absorb one another), owing
To the viscosity of the still-wet paints.

New shades of blue-green started playing there,
As I sat spell-bound, with my brush in hand,

But held away from the canvas so as not to interfere
With the wonder taking place as the shades went by.

Kaleidoscopic, they were: Going from one into another.
I wished, at times, to stop them—but knew I could do no

More than enjoy, and marvel. I will never be able to
Accurately guess at the number of shades that one stroke

Produced, but it was many; of that I can assure you.
And I watched until the oils found their final hue: A new

Blue-green! And, for an eternal second, they held together.
When I awoke I could still see that color. I look for it today.

The Pilgrimage

They speak of pilgrimage, of going to this place or that,
Seeking a mysterious adventure of discovery in a holy setting.

And yet pilgrimage is mixed with life, inseparably. Even if
You refuse to go it happens, in your cell, or on the mountain top.

There are various stopping-off points along the way.
Chance meetings will help to guide you; and you are going far.

A question of importance is whether you chose this route.
Like most vital questions it will not be answered—or will it?

The Road Home

It's time to take the thoughts out and dust them off.
So many paper-scraps, pencil or ink-stained.
(Did I write all that?)

A story unfurls as they scatter about the table top.
Pink and blue and white; and all shapes they are.
The days of dreams.

If one of those days were to be re-lived; Wonder!
That these words seemed, once, to tell about
The goings-on then.

And the goal; no closer now than ever.
Or an inch closer—which *is* a giant leap.
So far we've come . . .

And yet so far to go, as we make our pilgrimage.
Onward, with hopeful hearts, yearning for the place
Where first we lost our way.

The Road to Serendipity

Serendipity: We'll live there one day. Perhaps it's just at the end of
 boredom.
But there are many cold days, lost along the way. I know it's not a
 location, but a sensation.

And serendipity is not akin to hope. We might even be something
 else when we arrive there—
Depending upon what eats us.

And the trip just happens—all that's asked of you is to help break
 those chains, the ones put there by others along the way,
 and to keep your campfire stoked.

Or, it may lie at the culmination point; after a given amount of
 experience.
When you arrive you might know how you got there.

And when we're gone, I wonder what will grow to take our place
 in that new life?
We'll just go on, for now, and rev-up our own emotions.

The Truth about Truth

Amidst one mirthful moment,
When all seems frivolous and funny,
Comes an abiding feeling of gloom.

And again, out of nowhere,
A terrible sensation makes you smile;
And the world seems upside-down.

The truth is funny, yet scary at the same time.
And when those two words, funny and scary,
Fit together best; look for truth to be nearest.

The Unknowing Me

Tell me, please, it's me that's wrong:
That in my ignorance and pride I'm lost.

It just can't be that everything's so untrue.
This illusion is a passing thing, for sure.

Something I'll get over, like a strong disease;
But not chronic, terminal. Just a phase.

But I'm alright: Either way I'll survive.
In fact I'll flourish, bloom like a flower.

Because I know I'll come to my senses,
And see that I am not equipped to read

These tea-leaves; like the gurus and the pundits
And the preachers, and the masses, can.

So they will suffer for me; and I will
Recede into my little cave, for a while longer.

The Weight of the World

And you feel the world—
Oppressive.

Holding your body and soul
To the ground!

When all you ever wanted
Was to fly.

The Whole of Me

The whole of me, it seems,
Was scattered, then, among the several
Personalities I became as the years went by:
Some gone now and a few hanging on.

So much laughter; and misplaced anguish,
Make up a life so full of being a human, a man.
And, in the happy act-two, life goes out, slowly:
First the lies, then the eyes.

The Whole Truth

If, in fact,
The whole truth is
Ever really told,

It will be versed
In a poetic fashion;
(Where nothing is
Ever really told . . .)

The wisest man
On earth is one
Who knows nothing,

And so, he is the
Right one to compose,
Or discover, that poem.

And read it back;
First to himself,
And then, to the rest of us.

The Wisher of Wishes

I don't doubt much.
Everything imaginable is probably going to come about,
Somewhere, sometime.
And there is always enough time for wishes to come true:
In fact, time may be nothing more
Than the God-given duration we perceive between creation and
      experience;
Between dreaming and waking.
And time will go on for as long as there is someone caught up in
      the act of wishing, or dreaming.
For God loves the dreamer, and the wisher of wishes.

The Word Chest

Just some words, going nowhere: Not meant to mean anything, in
    particular.
Just some words that needed to get out of my head—There! Now they're
    gone.

More will take their place—they're already gathering; materializing, like
    ghosts.
The dead places they've come from, I can't know; can't even offer a good
    guess.

They come through all of us, the words, but only a few, like me, seem to
    need
To put them down for posterity—as if they're important little bits of
    treasure.

There must be a wooden chest somewhere, where all the words are kept.
    And
A keeper of the chest, who lets them out in some order, some priority, as
    needed.

Without the release of the old words would the lights go out in our brain,
    our soul?
It seems to me unreasonable to think that we, beings who have only
    confused

Themselves the more with the passing of time, could with any confidence
Think that we will invent new words, new thoughts, when the chest is
    empty.

So, to that extent, the words do seem to take on monumental value; real
    worth.
And putting them down, to save what we have been given so far,
    imperative.

Things I've Never Felt

I've never felt like a drummer in a band,
Keeping a steady tempo to a song that many sing.

I've never felt like a hero.
If, once in a while, I was one, it was only me being me.

I've never felt afraid to do, or think, something new:
The way to the truth is there.

I've never felt privileged,
Like I had something coming to me.

I've never felt self-sure,
Like I knew any real secrets.

This Old Taos House

The wind, blowing the tree branches around,
Interfered with the sun in just such a way that,
Through my window and onto the walls of my room,
The light made music; which I could faintly hear
In the silent shadows it cast.

This Road Leads Toward the Eternal Sea

The well-lived life winds down,
As we travel the road that descends
To the eternal sea.

No more climbing
Is in us—so we welcome that.
And we travel on,

Through the meadow,
Watching for the holes,
So as not to turn an ankle.

Yet looking upward,
Above the horizon,
To see the things

We couldn't see
While we were striving—or starving.
An answer to a prayer, yet unspoken.

Thoughts or Wild Horses?

Once again my thoughts go wandering.
They can be so much like a band of wild horses.

Grazing, they can focus. There,
They ruminate, but wistfully.

They seem to be looking around, taking
In a floating cloud.

And suddenly, without an apparent cause,
Hooves pound the ground, majestically!

(*They* know how wild, and free, they are.)
And they're off to summer pastures.

Time: The Great Illusion

How easily a day slips away,
A decade even quicker.
An hour can be forever,
A second like a flicker.

And one's bright human life,
Goes by in one long day.
Though many dreams passed by—
Observe, mankind, while you may.

Touched by the Mystery

Your world is moved,
The past is gone.
The Mercy has come,
To sing her song.

To each it comes,
Tho' some may not feel
The touch, so loving,
The touch that heals.

Unlikely

How amazingly unlikely everything is—
Even the things that *do* happen.

Thinking about something only makes me
Not (want to) do it.

So, I must find those things I can do,
Without thinking of them.

Maybe then . . .

Until Winter Comes

How fitting that we started
On a winter solstice morning.

Each year now the light has been
Getting brighter and brighter.

Now the spring has come, and
With it the warmth of an everlasting love.

Let us bask in the sunshine,
Until winter comes again.

Visitor in the Desert

Everywhere I look,
Things that belong here; not I?
To my way of seeing,
All these things,
The grasses, the cactus, the rocks;
They all live here—
While I am just a visitor,

Their guest; whether invited, tolerated or hated.
I'll stay, anyway,
For a time, and see what the feeling is
That comes from them.
I believe in their powers:
To expel me; or to help me prosper
In their company.

Warmth

Now you know you're heading in the right direction;
And away from the prison,

(Though a few things seemed comfortable enough.)
That new kind of warmth speaks to you.

At night, your body is afire from within.
Whereas, once, you would shiver,

Now you throw back the covers and laugh wildly!
Then dreams appear, always soft,

Tangled loosely with your love.
Even the chill of morning is welcomed by your heightened

Sensations. And, glancing back,
You see the road has vanished.

With no plan, no reason; and no explanation at all.
Just think where the road ahead might go.

Was the Buzz Worth This?

Outside the window
The pine trees are
Blown by the wind.

The journeys and
Adventures—the times
I had—come to another end.

There's been a plan—
But not my own—
At work all along.

Turning the tides
This way and that,
Composing a song.

And now it is
Written—but yet
Incomplete somehow.

More to be appended
Before it's all ended.

Watering the Weeds

While in the yard, watering the grass, the bushes, the flowers;
I come across a patch of weeds, dry from the sun, just like the others.
And I wondered, "Shall I put water on them—nourish these weeds?"

I understand the argument some folks may make: Sacrifice ugliness
And preserve the beautiful. Or, that the weeds impede the growth of
The lovely ones; those that please the senses and dazzle the eye.

But they are all green, are they not? And they all grow from the
Same soil as all the rest of nature's creations. Why neglect them, alone?
And so I directed the shower onto them; but *just a little*, though. . . .

If we were flora, would we be watered? Would the one who gives
Life to all things on earth see fit to water us well? Or are we just
Weeds? Perhaps that's why Nature has given mankind only *just a little*.

What Did I Do This Season?

In the midst of a late summer daydream,
I saw a pair of leaves falling outside my window.
And I thought of the end of the season.
"What did I do this season?"

Another season, unlike all the others,
And yet so similar in the way it flowed.
The emergence from winter, and onto a new path.
Idling in the summer shade.

Watching the water flow through the *acequia;*
Onward to where it was going, never to return.
The birds that came, and are now going elsewhere;
Some with new families, others without their mate.

And what did they do this season?
Everything.
Nothing left to be done now but to get ready for another winter.
Like the birds, I'll lovingly recall the season, and then go on.

What Do I Ask?

I've seen one of these, and one of those;
Throughout the known world, and beyond.

For each new thing I see, a different question evolves:
How much of everything have I seen, or even imagined, yet?

The questions come with the experience—each encounter brings
        its own.
Not searching: For I don't know what is out there.

In my weakest moments, and in painful times,
I play-act at knowledge, perhaps to feel safe, or wise, somehow.

At times I've been a singer, an actor, a dancer, a poet;
(Perhaps not as good as you). Being something else while time
        passed.

Having now accumulated so many questions, which ones do I ask;
Knowing that it will only be me who hears the answers?

Where Am I?

I awoke in a dream
To find myself in a strange place:
Stranger than the dream before.

I knew, in the way a dreamer can,
That this was a new place:
There were several moons.

It was cold and dark, I'm sure,
Although I did not feel cold;
And didn't miss the light.

I was consumed by memories
Of things I could not remember;
Yet the memories were lucid.

Like the dreams I was unsure of,
I was unsure of the memories—
Perhaps too far gone to place.

Where did I come from, and
Where was I going from here?
To the next place; which is still here?

Where Did the Ideal Go?

Where did it go,
That lovely hope that things were as they should be,
And always would be?

I struggled with it,
Like a lover. And it loved me back, too, in its way.
Until the other day,

When I looked for it,
Upon waking, and saw only a puff of smoke,
Going on its way.

That's all it was, anyhow.
An idea that saw me through the early days,
But it was just a play.

And now, without it, I find
That life is still going on; I am still me;
The world is still it.

And we'll all most likely, stay that way.

Where Life is Going

Life keeps marching onward;
Toward wherever it is going.

The future is not necessarily
Written; but then, it might be.

No need to do anything:
But look! Watch it moving. Feel it going on!

What great thing ever came about
Except in stages? And who are we,

To expect it to go our way?
Just live. That's what I'd say.

Who Are You?

Who are you?
Who are you that I am writing to?

And who am I to think that you might care?
Are you and I one, as I have often considered?

Or can each particle be separate?
I want to believe all is one, but can't all the time.

And can't we measure our own truths, at least somewhat,
By how long they stay with us; or how often they visit?

I will continue to address you; I hope you won't mind.
My audience has always been my last consideration.

Why Did Love Go?

Why did love have to go away?
I think I can recall the very day.
Was it replaced by something?

Maybe time?

Love's wound healed,
And now scarred over;
Only a memory.

Wind, Clouds and Mountain

Once they were separate,
But now the wind and clouds

Descend upon the mountain.
And the wind becomes

The mountain's wind.
And the clouds,

The mountain's clouds.
And the mountain,

The wind's, and the cloud's.
And, all of them, The Mountain God's.

Wisps of Thought

All those thoughts,
Or messages,

Have now gone back
To where they came from

In the beginning.
Having cycled through

So many, many other's
Senses, in just as many

Forms of language.
Now my touch is upon them

As they stray through space,
On their way around again.

The imagination
Is the unreal.

And so, in every unreal thought,
Imagination is at work.

Illusion is the world
Of imagination.

Without Secrets

And, one day, your eyes grow bigger—
Your nose, too; and your hearing piques.

You can experience so much more of life!
So much you've wished for—now yours.

But all too soon, your big eyes are flooded;
You smell the stench of far-off populations,

And the cacophony of conflict and competitions.
You want to return to your original limitations.

Now you know—you were only being protected.
Without secrets there is so little happiness.

Yellow Lustre

The high prairie is showing its life,
In yellow patches.
Growing up in splotches, here and there,
Though it's late September.
They surround us as we walk the dusty,
Climbing, rocky path;
Where we can look out
Upon the sea of tumbleweeds
That stretches right out to the open sky beyond.

www.ingramcontent.com/pod-product-compliance
Lightning Source LLC
Chambersburg PA
CBHW021405090426
42742CB00009B/1007